Mastering Media

The News
Never Stops

John DiConsiglio

Chicago, Illinois

www.heinemannraintree.com
Visit our website to find out more information about Heinemann-Raintree books.

To order:
☎ Phone 888-454-2279
💻 Visit www.heinemannraintree.com
to browse our catalog and order online.

© 2011 Raintree
an imprint of Capstone Global Library, LLC
Chicago, Illinois

Visit our website at
www.heinemannraintree.com

Edited by Adam Miller, Andrew Farrow, and Adrian Vigliano
Designed by Steve Mead
Original illustrations © Capstone Global Library Ltd.
Picture research by Elizabeth Alexander
Production by Alison Parsons
Originated by Capstone Global Library Ltd
Printed and bound in China by South China Printing Company Ltd.

14 13 12 11 10
10 9 8 7 6 5 4 3 2

Library of Congress Cataloging-in-Publication Data
DiConsiglio, John.
    The News Never Stops / John DiConsiglio.
        p. cm. — (Mastering Media)
    Includes bibliographical references and index.
    ISBN 978-1-4109-3843-5 (hardcover)
    1. Journalism—United States.
    2. Broadcast journalism—United States.
    I. Title.
    PN4888.B74D33 2010
    071'.3—dc22

2010003543

Acknowledgments
We would like to thank the following for permission to reproduce photographs: Alamy pp. **12** (© Chuck Mason), **30** (© Irene Abdou), **35** (© Boitano Photography), **42** (© NetPics); Corbis pp. **6** (© H. Armstrong Roberts/ClassicStock), **10** (© Bettmann), **16** (© Toby Melville/Reuters), **18** (© Corbis), **20 right** (© Bettmann), **26** (© Corbis), **29** (© Mark Peterson), **36** (© Rick Maiman/Sygma), **38** (© Andy Rain/epa), **39 top** (© Rune Hellestad), **39 bottom** (© Peter Foley/epa); Getty Images pp. **4** (Joe Raedle), **7** (Ralph Crane/Time & Life Pictures), **8** (Boris Horvat/AFP), **15** (Hulton Archive), **20 left** (Hulton Archive), **21** (David Hume Kennerly), **22** (John Moore), **24** (Arthur Cofod/Pictures Inc./Time Life Pictures), **32** (NASA/AFP), **34** (CBS Photo Archive), **44** (CAREL PEDRE/AFP), **46** (SHADISHD173/AFP), **48** (Dan Kitwood); Photolibrary pp. **19** (Norbert Michalke/imagebroker.net), **40** (Carlos Cazalis/arabianEye); © Yousef A. Raffah p. **47**.

Cover photograph of a US tank destroyed in Baghdad, reproduced with permission of Getty Images/Mirrorpix.

We would like to thank Devorah Heitner for her invaluable help in the preparation of this book.

Every effort has been made to contact copyright holders of any material reproduced in this book. Any omissions will be rectified in subsequent printings if notice is given to the publisher.

Disclaimer
All the Internet addresses (URLs) given in this book were valid at the time of going to press. However, due to the dynamic nature of the Internet, some addresses may have changed, or sites may have changed or ceased to exist since publication. While the author and publisher regret any inconvenience this may cause readers, no responsibility for any such changes can be accepted by either the author or the publisher.

Contents

Some words are printed in bold, **like this**. You can find out what they mean by looking in the glossary.

Breaking News

Dateline 1990

You are a reporter with a **scoop**—a news story you will be the first to report. You are in Baghdad on the eve of the first Gulf War (1990–91). U.S. missiles bombard the Iraqi capital. On a rooftop overlooking the city, your cameraman trains a lens on you. Millions of people around the world switch on their televisions. They watch you report on the war as bombs explode behind you.

Dateline 2005

You are a reporter with a scoop. Three bombs have exploded on London's subway trains. An hour later, a double-decker bus is bombed. You are the first to interview police on the scene. You quickly write up your notes. Your report will appear in tomorrow's edition of the *New York Times*—and almost immediately on the newspaper's website.

Dateline 2010

You are a reporter with a scoop. You have heard that a famous athlete has failed a drug test. You click on your computer and quickly post the rumor on your Internet **blog**. In less than a second, it is available around the world for people to read on computers and on "smartphones" like iPhones and BlackBerries. It sets off a flurry of posts on social networking sites like Facebook and Twitter.

Welcome to the world of 24-hour news.

As these examples show, the way news is reported has changed remarkably in recent history. The changes over the last few centuries have been even greater. From the printed page to television cameras to the Internet, technology has transformed news-gathering, as well as the news itself.

The telegraph

Until the 1840s, most news traveled no faster than a horse or a ship. The **telegraph**, an electric wire that carried messages the same way phone lines do, sped things up greatly. But even then, it often took days or weeks for news to reach readers.

Newspapers and magazines were the leading news sources of the time. When the passenger ship the *Titanic* sunk in 1912, only one newspaper carried accounts of the disaster—and it was more than a day after it happened.

Reporters rushed to make newspaper deadlines in the early 1900s, but news still traveled slowly.

The revolution of radio and television

By the 1920s, radio revolutionized the news **industry**. People switched the dial on the radios in their living rooms and heard staticky descriptions of world events as they happened. In the 1950s, television brought the sounds and pictures of the news into homes.

TV revolutionized the news industry. Suddenly, the world could see news events, like this press conference from President John F. Kennedy.

"Radio and television gave you an immediacy [sense of being there] that you never had before," says Ohio University **journalism** professor Patrick Washburn. "Suddenly you could be anywhere in the country and if you could see a television, the news came to life for you."

The rise of the Internet

In the late 1990s and 2000s, the Internet plugged the news into a whole new world. With websites, blogs, and social networking services like Twitter, news is now available all the time. Today, anyone with Internet access can be wired into almost unlimited sources of news.

What is news?

But what is news, exactly? Charles A. Dana, a **journalist** from the 1800s, defined it as "Anything that interests a large part of the community and has never been brought to its attention before." In other words, news is new. It is what people are talking about. UK writer Evelyn Waugh said, "News is what the chap who doesn't care much about anything wants to read."

Journalism is the reporting of news. Traditional journalism—whether it is a newspaper article or a television report—is based on the "five W's": who, what, where, when, and why. Those are the five most important questions in a news story. A journalist should answer those questions within the first paragraph of an article or, on television, within the first few seconds of a report.

Public scenes of reporters fighting for a statement only represent a small part of the journalism process.

Avoiding bias

In theory, journalists are taught to never take sides on an issue. They are trained to tell the story exactly as it happened. But not all stories are reported equally or from the same perspective. Reporters can have a **bias**, meaning they support one point of view, based on the type of news they report and the kind of **media**, or news outlet, they work for (see box below).

How does bias work?

To understand how bias works, let's look at a case of a famous athlete who is accused of failing a drug test for steroids. An army of reporters might pounce on the story. But each one could see it from a different angle.

- A news reporter might seek out the facts: When was the athlete caught? What was the drug he used? Is the test reliable?
- A sports reporter might focus on the impact on the athlete's team: Will he be suspended? For how long? How will his team replace him?
- A financial reporter might look at the economic outcome of the story: Will the athlete be fined? Will he lose his shoe company contract? What will happen to the team's ticket sales?
- And an entertainment reporter could look at the more personal side of the story: What does the athlete's movie star wife think? Will they still attend exclusive parties? Does the public still like them?

In each case, the reporters are doing their jobs, and they are probably trying their best to tell the truth. But they are delivering the news to different audiences—news seekers, sports fans, money managers, and star-watchers. They tailor their reports to fit those audiences.

News or gossip?

Throughout the history of journalism, reporters have not always been able to keep bias out of their stories.

🌐 A journalist's code of ethics

Journalists should follow a certain code of ethics, or rules. These rules include:

• Seek the truth and report it fully.

• Look for different perspectives. In other words, report on all sides of an issue.

• Do not report on any story if you have a personal connection to it. For example, if it involves your friends or family or a group that you belong to.

• Do not be influenced by anything but the truth. Do not let powerful people change your mind, and do not accept gifts from anyone.

TO THE

Tradesmen, Mechanics, &c.

OF THE PROVINCE OF

Pennsylvania.

MY DEAR AND MUCH RESPECTED BRETHREN,

AT a Time when a corrupt and proflituted Miniftry are pointing their deftructive Machines against the facred Liberties of the *Americans*, the Eyes of all *Europe* are upon us; and much is expected from the known Refolution and Conduct of the *Pennfylvanians*, amongft whom the induftrious and refpectable Body of TRADESMEN and MECHANICS bear a very large Proportion. The Point in Queftion is, Whether we have Property of our own, or not? whether our Property, and the dear-earned Fruits of our Labour, are at our own Difpofal, or fhall be wantonly wrefted from us, by a Set of luxurious, abandoned, and piratical Hirelings, to be appropriated by them to increafe the Number of fuch infamous Penfioners, and fupport their unlimited Extravagance? The Refult depends on our determined Virtue and Integrity, at fo important a Crifis.

THE Nature of the deteftable TEA-SCHEME, and the pernicious Confequences of fubmitting to receive IT amongft us, fubjected to a Duty payable here, and levied on us without our Confent, have been fo judicioufly fet forth, and demonftrated by abler Pens, as to leave no Room for one of my Capacity to undertake it; and, if the trifling Duty of *Three Pence* were ONLY to be confidered, it would not be worth our while to oppofe it; nor worth while for the Miniftry to ftrenuoufly to infift on. and take off, in Lieu thereof, a much greater Sum payable in *London*: But, that by this Breach (though fmall, they will enter the Bulwark of our facred Liberties, and will never defift, till they have made a Conqueft of the Whole.

THESE arbitrary Meafures we have virtuoufly oppofed hitherto: Let us for our own Sakes, for our Pofterity's Sake, for our Country's Sake, ftedfaftly perfevere in oppofing to the End. Corruption, Extravagance, and Luxury, are feldom found in the Habitations of Tradefmen. Induftry, Œconomy, Prudence, and Fortitude, generally inhabit there; and I expect to fee thefe commendable Virtues fhine forth upon the prefent Occafion, with more than brilliant Luft

LET not the artful Infinuation of our Enemies, *That the Duty will be paid in England, by the Eaft-India Company, and not in America,* have any Weight amongft us: This is one of their Toils to enfnare us. The Act of 11th of GEO. 3, exprefsly lays the aforefaid *Duty,* on all Teas imported in *America* from *England,* payable on its landing here: And no private Contract between the *Eaft India* Company and the Lords of the Treafury, no Power under the Crown, nor even the King himfelf, can difpenfe with, fet afide, difannul, or make void fuch a Claufe, or any other in any Act of Parliament, but the fame Power and Authority by which it was enacted The grand Point in View is, by every Artifice to enflave the *American* Colonies, and to plunder them of their Property, and, what is more, *their Birth-Right,* LIBERTY. It is therefore highly incumbent on us unitedly, with Heart and Soul, to refift the diabolical Delufion, and defpife the infamous Penfioners

BUT fuppofing the Act was repealed, and the Tea could be imported free of any Duty, Impoft, or Cuftom; yet, is it not a moft grofs and daring Infult to pilfer the Trade from the *Americans,* and lodge it in the Hands of the *Eaft-India* Company? Let us not be prevailed upon to fuppofe that this will affect the Merchants only:——We need not concern ourfelves with it:——It will firft moft fenfibly affect the Merchants; but it will alfo very materially affect YOU, ME, and every Member of the Community. The *Eaft-India* Company at prefent have fhipped their defperate Adventure in chartered Bottoms; it was prudent fo to do, or elfe poffibly their obnoxious Veffels and Cargoes might become a Sacrifice to the Refentment of a much injured and exafperated People. The fame Confideration might probably have induced them to appoint our Merchants their Agents to fupport the firft heat of Action, rightly judging that if we would enfnare our Friends *with Whigs*, we fhould chaftife their Factors *with Scorpions.* But if they can once open the Channel of Trade to themfelves, they will hereafter fhip their Teas in their own Bottoms. They have paffed a grofs Affront upon our Merchants in appointing fuch, whom we refpect, Commiffioners. Hereafter, if they fucceed, they will fend their own Factors and Creatures, eftablifh Houfe, amongft US Ship US all other *Eaft-India* Goods; and in order to full freight their Ships, take in other Kind of Goods at under Freight, or (more probably) fhip them on their own Accounts to their own Factors, and under fell our Merchants, till they monopolize the whole Trade. Thus our Merchants are ruined, Ship Building ceafes. They will then fell Goods at any exorbitant Price. Our Artifice. will be unemployed, and every Tradefman will groan under the dire Oppreffion.

THE *Eaft India* Company, if once they get Footing in this (once) happy Country, will leave no Stone unturned to become your Mafters. They are an opulent Body, and Money or Credit is not wanting amongft them. They have a defigning, depraved, and defpotic Miniftry to affift and fupport them. They themfelves are well verfed in TYRANNY, PLUNDER, OPPRESSION, and BLOODSHED. Whole Provinces labouring under the Diftreffes of Oppreffion, Slavery, Famine, and the Sword, are familiar to them. Thus they have enriched themfelves,—thus they are become the moft powerful Trading Company in the Univerfe. Be, therefore, my dear Fellow-Tradefmen, prudent,——be watchful,—be determined to let no Motive induce you to favour the accurfed Scheme. Reject every Propofal, but a *repealing Act.* Let not their baneful Commodity enter YOUR City. Treat every Aidor or Abettor with Ignominy, Contempt, &c. and let YOUR whole Deportment prove to the World, "THAT WE WILL BE FREE INDEED."

A MECHANIC.

Philadelphia, December 4, 1773.

📧 This 1773 colonial newspaper printed criticism of British taxes instead of unbiased news.

In the 1700s, European newspapers were generally fair. But some people used printed documents to argue for specific causes. Puritan John Milton distributed pamphlets opposing religious discrimination. And Jonathan Swift, the author of *Gulliver's Travels*, printed attacks on Britain's abuse of the poor.

Journalism barely existed in the United States before the American Revolution (1775–83). The earliest printed news was mostly gossip and opinions. Many newspapers and pamphlets were designed to spread political ideas.

In 1721 James Franklin and his little brother Benjamin started the newspaper the *New-England Courant*. It had little actual news, but its fiery opinions helped sway Americans in favor of revolution. Even Benjamin Franklin admitted that "the business of printing has chiefly to do with men's opinions."

Just the facts

The next century saw a more traditional news world, one in which reporters—or newspapers, radio stations, and television networks—were expected to stick to the facts. However, as we will see, bias still often creeps into all kinds of reporting.

 Libel

What happens when a journalist lies? That is called **libel**. And it can cause a lot of damage to a journalist's career and reputation.

What can people do if they think a journalist has "libeled" them? Let's go back to the athlete who tests positive for steroids (see page 9). What if the reporter was wrong, and the athlete never failed the drug test? The athlete could sue the reporter for libel and take her to court. If the athlete won the case, he could collect a lot of money from the reporter and her employer, whether it is a newspaper, television station, or website.

But libel can be very hard to prove. The athlete would have to show that the reporter lied on purpose, and that she did so to harm the athlete. If the athlete could not prove those points, he would lose his case.

Newspapers and Magazines Change the Media World

Roll the presses! Newspapers are still produced on giant printing presses.

U.S. President Thomas Jefferson once said that if he had a choice between government without newspapers or newspapers without government, he would pick the newspapers, hands down.

More than 200 years later, newspapers are still, in many ways, the backbone of **journalism**.

Before radio, television, and eventually the Internet, newspapers were the fastest way to spread word of major events. For example, when an earthquake rocked San Francisco in 1906, readers around the world read the details about it in their newspapers, although not until nearly a week later. At the time, that was considered fast-moving news!

Throughout the rest of the century, people across the world depended on their daily paper to catch up on **global** events. Today, many people are still used to finding a newspaper on their doorsteps every morning or buying them as they travel to work.

Watchdogs and crusaders

There are many different kinds of newspaper and magazine **journalists**, as we will see in this chapter. Many of them often see themselves as watchdogs. They keep an eye on governments and powerful people to make sure they are not abusing their roles. From South America to South Africa, reporters have **crusaded** for public freedoms.

Crusading can be dangerous for all types of journalists. A nonprofit group called Reporters Without Borders supports the rights of the **press** all over the globe. The organization reports that in 2009 alone, 76 journalists were killed and 573 imprisoned for their work. Most often, journalists face these dangers in poor countries or those without a strong tradition of freedom of the press.

The "Penny Press"

In the 1800s, the popularity of U.S. and European newspapers rose dramatically. The Industrial Revolution, a period when machines and factories began to be widely used, was flourishing. This meant papers could be printed quickly and cheaply. A new postal system meant that newspapers were also easier to deliver. The invention of the **telegraph** allowed reporters to rapidly relay news to their paper's headquarters.

In 1833 Benjamin Day opened the *New York Sun*. It was the first "**Penny Press**"—a cheap daily newspaper. The "Pennies" drew readers with **sensational** reports on murders, sex, and **scandals**. The number of U.S. newspapers skyrocketed from 3,000 in 1860 to 7,000 in 1880. Big cities like New York and Chicago had as many as 10 newspapers that reached 15 million people.

Yellow journalism

As newspapers grew, reporters fiercely tracked stories to feed the public's growing appetite for news. Some stories were spectacular, such as reports on the 1906 San Francisco earthquake or the 1912 sinking of the *Titanic*. Others were sensational, focusing on famous people's love affairs.

In New York City, two rival **publishers** used their newspapers to change public opinion—and make themselves rich. At the turn of the century, William Randolph Hearst's *New York Journal* helped create U.S. support for the Spanish–American War (1898). "War is good for **circulation** [the number of readers]," he said.

Across town, Joseph Pulitzer's *New York World* crusaded for the poor. Pulitzer attracted readers with wild headlines. For example, a story on a heat wave was titled "How Babies Are Baked." Both publishers practiced "**yellow journalism**," a style of writing that stresses eye-catching headlines and sensational details over hard facts.

Lord Beaverbrook

In the United Kingdom during the same period, William Maxwell Aitken (also known as Lord Beaverbrook) was an early star of "Fleet Street." The UK press got this nickname from the name of the street where it had its offices. In the early 1900s, Beaverbrook transformed dull newspapers into witty, colorful journals with eye-catching photo layouts.

William Maxwell Aitken (Lord Beaverbrook) was England's first media baron. In the early 1900s, he transformed dull newspapers into colorful journals.

Muckraking

In the early 1900s, many writers used their newspapers and magazines to expose government **corruption** and highlight unfair treatment of workers. They attacked big business and child labor abuses. U.S. President Theodore Roosevelt named them **"muckrakers."** He said they never raised their head from the "muck" of the floor while searching tirelessly for wrongdoing to expose.

After World War I (1914–18), Beaverbrook's *Daily Express* was the most widely read newspaper in the world. Beaverbrook could make or break famous people by the way he instructed reporters in his newspapers to report a story.

15

Tabloid times

In 1952 Italian publisher Generoso Pope bought a horse-racing newspaper called the *National Enquirer*. He instantly shifted its focus from horses to horrors. He ran sleazy stories about gruesome murders and grisly deeds, with headlines like "I Cut out Her Heart and Stomped on It!" and "I Ate My Baby!" The *Enquirer's* circulation quickly jumped to a million copies a week.

The **tabloid** era was off to the races. Tabloid newspapers were named for the large size of their pages. Taking yellow journalism one step further, they combined breaking news stories with celebrity gossip. Then and today, tabloids frequently report on the sex scandals of the rich and famous.

Tabloids like Britain's *Sun* have high circulation by combining news with gossip and scandals.

What a scoop!

But the tabloids are not just fluff. Reporters working for tabloids regularly get a **scoop** before more traditional journalists, and they expose public corruption and private problems. For example, in 2007, tabloids reported rumors that U.S. presidential candidate John Edwards had an affair and fathered a child outside his marriage. The story, which turned out to be true, was not picked up by other **media** until two years later. In 2008, tabloids reported that pop star Michael Jackson was gravely ill—only a matter of months before his death in 2009.

Is it news?

But are tabloids, with their focus on the sleazy and sensational, really news?

Many "mainstream" journalists would say no. They note that tabloids report on issues that may be popular with the public, but that are not really newsworthy. They also argue that, unless someone is breaking the law, the private lives of even celebrities should remain private.

Tabloids have famously followed, even harassed, celebrities in search of scoops. Britain's Princess Diana was often surrounded by packs of tabloid reporters and photographers nicknamed "paparazzi." When she was killed in a Paris car accident while being chased by photo-seeking paparazzi, Britain's three leading tabloids admitted they were partially to blame. Tabloid coverage had, as the **editor** of the UK *Sun* put it, "created a frenzy and appetite around Diana" that helped contribute to her death.

But tabloid editors say they are just giving the public what it wants by aggressively pursuing stories that other journalists ignore. This is perhaps proven by the fact that tabloids are widely successful. *The Sun* has the highest circulation of any English-language daily newspaper in the world.

In the last 100 years, newsrooms have changed from cramped offices with click-clacking typewriter keys...

Inside the newsroom

Take a peek inside a busy newsroom. It is where news gathering begins. Reporters scurry from desk to desk. Editors bark out orders. The click-clack of typing fills the air.

But is this a scene from 2010 or 1910?

Sure, newsrooms have changed a lot in the last 100 years. Today's reporters write on computer keyboards—not typewriter keys. Televisions and Internet connections are on every desk. Almost all newspapers have their own websites. And while most staff members are still men, more than 30 percent of today's reporters are women.

But some things are still the same. At most newspapers, reporters sit at desks, collecting news and writing articles. Their stories are passed on to editors who review and even rewrite them. The editors also work with photographers, designers, and illustrators. These people work on the images that accompany a story and create the overall appearance of the newspaper.

Editorials

Flip through a newspaper. There are different sections for different topics: front-page news, fashion, business, sports, and more. Writers for all of these sections are expected to follow the journalism tradition of not being **biased**.

But that is not true for the whole newspaper. Most newspapers set aside columns called "editorials." These articles are not supposed to be about listing facts. They express the views of the editors or owners. They state the newspaper's official opinion on important issues, such as who they think should win an upcoming election.

... to modern newsrooms, equipped with computers, TVs, and state-of-the-art technology.

Climbing the pyramid

Imagine a newspaper article as an upside-down pyramid. At the top are the most important facts of the story: the five W's, or who, what, where, when, and why. The details at the bottom, the pyramid's point, are less critical. That is the way that newspaper reporters are taught to write. It is a style called the inverted pyramid.

Why do they write like this? One theory is that busy readers do not have time to finish a whole story. All of the meaty news must be in the beginning. Others say that editors came up with the idea so they could easily cut articles that run too long. They would just have to chop off the fluff at the pyramid's point. And some say the style came from the telegraph. Before phones, reporters used the electrical wires to transmit stories to their editors. But telegraphs were unreliable. The most vital facts had to be relayed first, before the signal was lost.

19

HEADLINERS:
THE NAMES THAT MADE NEWSPAPER HISTORY

Here are a few of the biggest names in newspaper history.

UPTON SINCLAIR

Upton Sinclair's 1906 muckraking book, *The Jungle*, uncovered horrific conditions in Chicago's meatpacking **industry**. Sinclair found that companies sold dirty and diseased food to the public. His book led to the first food safety and consumer protection laws.

PERCY HOSKINS

The lead crime reporter for the UK newspaper the *Daily Express*, Percy Hoskins covered the 1956 trial of John Bodkin Adams, a suspected serial killer who was thought to have murdered as many as 400 people. Hoskins believed Adams was innocent. But no one else did, including Hoskins's publisher, Lord Beaverbrook himself (see page 15). Beaverbrook considered firing Hoskins, until Adams was found not guilty of the crimes.

ERNIE PYLE

Ernie Pyle traveled across the United States writing stories about ordinary people doing heroic things. His folksy style made him the most beloved journalist of his time. During World War II (1939–45), Pyle profiled soldiers in Europe and the Pacific and even followed them into battle. On one assignment with troops in the Pacific, Pyle was shot and killed by Japanese soldiers.

ETHEL PAYNE

When Ethel Payne was a dedicated reporter

for the *Chicago Defender*, a leading African American newspaper, she was given the nickname "First Lady of the Black Press." Payne fiercely supported civil rights for black people. She was a tough questioner and often angered U.S. presidents like Dwight Eisenhower. When the Civil Rights Act of 1964 was passed, President Lyndon Johnson invited Payne to attend the law's signing.

Bob Woodward (left) and Carl Bernstein (right).

BOB WOODWARD AND CARL BERNSTEIN

Perhaps the most famous journalists ever are Bob Woodward and Carl Bernstein, determined reporters who worked for the *Washington Post* in the 1970s. Woodward and Bernstein uncovered corruption and crimes in U.S. President Richard Nixon's administration and wrote about it in the *Post*. The scandal that resulted, called the Watergate scandal, led to the unthinkable: Nixon became the only U.S. president to ever resign from office.

SEYMOUR HERSH

Investigative reporter Seymour Hersh broke an important story during the Vietnam War (1955–75). In 1968 a group of U.S. soldiers marched into a small South Vietnamese town called My Lai. Looking for spies, the soldiers killed 500 women and children. Hersh broke the story to an outraged U.S. public.

He continues to make headlines today. In 2004, as the United States invaded Iraq, Hersh reported that U.S. soldiers were torturing captured Iraqis at a prison called Abu Ghraib. Hersh's report resulted in multiple trials and convictions of these soldiers.

Are newspapers dying?

Newspapers were once the fastest way to learn about world events.

Today, they seem as slow as the horse and buggy. There is little news on the front page that has not already been covered by television news or websites.

From the dawn of radio in the 1920s to the beginnings of television in the 1950s to the explosion of the Internet in the 1990s, experts have asked: Has technology left newspapers behind?

The final issue of Denver's *Rocky Mountain News*. The newspaper closed in 2009 after 150 years in the business.

Changing times

Many newspapers are losing money, readers, and staff. More than 50 U.S. newspapers, including the *Los Angeles Times* and *Chicago Tribune*, went bankrupt from 2008 to 2009. Denver's *Rocky Mountain News* closed in 2009 after 150 years. Americans under 30 are now twice as likely to get their news from television or the Internet as they are from newspapers.

Europeans are buying fewer newspapers, too. Circulation fell in 13 European nations in 2009, with the biggest drops in Ireland and the United Kingdom.

Some experts worry that a public without newspapers will be badly informed. They wonder what will happen if newspapers are not around to keep an eye on governments. Internet news and **blogs**, critics say, are filled with gossip rather than real reporting. (For more on this topic, see pages 43 to 47.)

New strategies

Still, newspapers are not giving up just yet. Newspaper sales are up in developing nations and new markets. China has recently seen a 4 percent boost in its newspaper growth. India's newspaper circulation went up almost 9 percent from 2004 to 2009.

Almost all newspapers have websites, most of which attract more readers than their print versions. More than 75 million people visit newspaper websites. Web audiences for newspapers around the world have grown by 350 percent in the period from about 2004 to 2009.

But while the Internet has offered new readers, newspapers have not figured out how to make money online. The Internet versions of newspapers are usually available for free. Worldwide, newspapers make just 2 percent of their money from the Internet.

"I have no doubt that there's still an appetite for the convenience of newspapers," says Helen Boaden, head of news for the British Broadcasting Company (BBC). "People are still going to want information, but newspapers are going to have to find new and innovative ways of getting to them."

Over the Airwaves

When the *Hindenburg* burst into flames in 1937, people around the world heard the news immediately on the radio.

In 1937 a giant German airship called the *Hindenburg* was completing a flight across the Atlantic Ocean. As it attempted to land near New Jersey, it suddenly exploded. The *Hindenburg* burst into flames, killing 35 passengers.

The news of the disaster spread immediately—but not by newspapers. Millions heard the *Hindenburg* crash as it happened. They heard it on the dominant **media** of the era: radio.

Rise of radio

By the late 1920s, radio had matched newspapers as the most important source of news. When the decade began, almost no homes had radios. By 1929, 40 percent of all Americans owned radios, and more than 5 million radios were sold every year.

In the United Kingdom, in 1922 the BBC was the first company to **broadcast** experimental radio programs. Early radio listeners had to purchase a "license" that helped fund the BBC.

At first, most radio broadcasts involved music and sports. The public tuned in to hear jazz singers like Al Jolson or listen to immensely popular 15-minute comedy shows.

But in the 1930s and 1940s, radio emerged as a source of instant world news. The BBC led the rise of news radio, following its **motto** to "inform, educate, and entertain." Instead of waiting for a morning newspaper, listeners now only had to turn on their radio.

Soon politicians and world leaders took advantage of the new medium. In the United Kingdom, King George V started the tradition of delivering a "Christmas message" to the country over the radio. His son George VI used a yearly radio speech to boost people's spirits during World War II.

In the United States, President Franklin D. Roosevelt used regular radio addresses, known as "fireside chats," to talk directly to the public. It helped him lead the country during the Great Depression (1929–c.1939) and World War II. Most people learned about Roosevelt's death in 1945 from a breaking news radio report.

Radio goes to war

The scene is London, 1940. The sky is filled with bomb flashes and billows of smoke. Warning sirens cut through the night. Nazi Germany is bombing the city. It is called the Blitz, and it will last for 57 straight nights. More than 43,000 people will be killed. Millions of homes will be destroyed.

And you are there—sort of. From a rooftop high above the city, CBS News radio reporter Edward R. Murrow is describing the Blitz in gripping detail. Listeners around the world are glued to their radios.

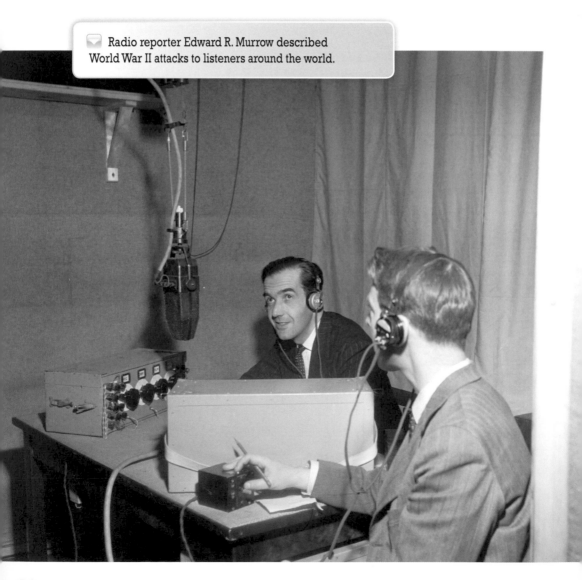

Radio reporter Edward R. Murrow described World War II attacks to listeners around the world.

Bringing the war home

Radio news reached its heights during World War II. Unlike newspapers, radio provided immediate coverage of world events. Murrow led the way. He reported on German leader Adolf Hitler's rage across Europe, and listeners followed his every step on their radios.

The propaganda wars

Even early on, radio was used for more than carrying news. Governments employed radio shows as **propaganda**, meaning the broadcasts were meant to influence public opinion.

During World War II, both sides beamed propaganda over the radio. (The two sides of the war were the Axis powers, made up of Germany, Japan, and Italy, versus the Allies, made up of Great Britain, the United States, France, the Soviet Union, and others.) On the Axis side, Germany and Japan used the airwaves to spread messages against the Allies. Japanese radio beamed messages from a broadcaster named "Tokyo Rose." "Rose" was really 12 separate female broadcasters who tried to disrupt Allied spirits by predicting their gruesome deaths. Germany used the voice of a woman nicknamed "Axis Sally" to taunt homesick Allied soldiers by saying their families had deserted them. She mocked the important D-Day invasion by telling Allied forces, "The D of D-Day stands for 'doom'...'disaster'...'death'...'defeat.'"

At the same time, the BBC broadcast messages of support to Allied troops throughout Europe. Announcers even sent code words to give instructions to Allied soldiers.

The new airwaves

Radio was the king of news media. But its reign did not last long. In the 1950s, television signaled the death of radio as the world's number-one news source. Suddenly the public would not settle for hearing events. It wanted to see them, too. (See pages 32 to 41 for more on television.)

Radio survived by specializing. Many stations changed from news stations to "Top 40" music channels and sports channels. In the 1960s and 1970s, BBC stations refused to play popular rock and roll music. As a result, hundreds of "pirate" radio stations beamed rock to UK radios. When the government tried to curtail their broadcasts, the "pirates" set up portable transmitters on boats.

But the news did maintain a presence on the radio. Today, the BBC still provides radio broadcasts to 182 million people around the world across 33 language services.

The Fairness Doctrine

The news has also remained relevant on the radio through a format called talk radio. In 1949 a U.S. law called the Fairness Doctrine had required stations to broadcast both sides of a **controversial** issue. If a commentator supported something such as a new law, his station had to give equal airtime to someone who was against it.

But opponents argued that the Fairness Doctrine violated free speech laws. The doctrine was **repealed** in 1987. Suddenly, radio talkers could say almost anything they wanted. Talk radio became a very popular way to discuss the news. Today, **partisan** voices (voices that support a particular point of view) fill the airwaves, pushing political opinions, often in harsh tones.

The rise of talk radio

Critics say that talk radio is less a place for news than a screaming match. Rush Limbaugh, the most successful talk radio pioneer, has famously attacked Democrats like President Bill Clinton and Barack Obama to an audience of 14.25 million listeners. Limbaugh's success opened the door for other opinionated radio hosts, like Bill O'Reilly (another conservative) and Al Franken (a liberal).

But talk radio's supporters claim they provide a **forum** for alternative views. By letting listeners call in, the shows open the airwaves to the public. There is no disputing talk radio's popularity. Today, 20 percent of Americans say they regularly listen to talk radio.

Rush Limbaugh's popularity as a radio personality has led to him having a powerful influence over conservative U.S. politics.

Radio Africa

Today's most thriving radio market is not in the United States or Europe. It is in Africa. Countries throughout the African continent are discovering that radio can be an important source of news, education, and even propaganda.

In many developing African nations, television is an expensive luxury. Newspaper delivery systems are often poor, and they reach only a small percentage of people—many of whom cannot read. But experts say radios can be found throughout African villages and cities.

A group of young people in Burkina Faso display their radio.

Propaganda airwaves

The BBC's African stations beam news reports around the world. Local channels play mixes of music, news, and call-in shows.

African governments have also used radio stations as propaganda tools, not unlike European radio during World War II. In Liberia, dictator Charles Taylor gave radio broadcasts to keep his "iron fist" rule over the country in the 1980s. In Rwanda in 1994, government announcers encouraged the elite to kill people from other ethnic groups. These announcements helped spark violence that led to the killings of over 500,000 Rwandans.

Uniting nations

Today, some African nations are using the airwaves to help unite their people. A loosening of government restrictions has allowed Somalia to develop a small network of private and community radio stations. These stations are important communication tools in a country where many people cannot read and there are few newspapers.

In Sierra Leone, radio pioneers are using the airwaves to heal the wounds of the nation's decades-long civil war. Radio led the way in rebuilding the country's infrastructure in 2000. Sierra Leone had only three stations. But that quickly grew into more than 20 stations. Today, 85 percent of the population relies on radio for news.

Radio played a huge role in Sierra Leone's 2002 elections, the country's first free elections in decades. Radio commentators gave information about polling locations and acted as watchdogs for violence and voting problems.

Television Takes Over

Astronaut Neil Armstrong took "One giant leap for mankind" when he walked on the Moon. Back on Earth, half a billion people watched him on TV.

It is July 1969. The impossible is happening. A spaceship has landed on the Moon. A U.S. astronaut named Neil Armstrong walks along the dusty surface. "One small step for man," Armstrong says. "One giant leap for mankind."

Half a billion people are witnesses, from more than 322,000 kilometers (200,000 miles) away. Back on Earth, an awed public huddles around millions of television sets to watch Armstrong's lunar landing. The age of television is in full swing.

Sights and sounds

The first television sets arrived in homes in the 1930s. But technical problems and high costs kept them from being widespread until the late 1940s. In 1949, about 1 million television sets were in U.S. homes. By 1950, there were 5 million. By 1959, more than 42 million houses had televisions. Many houses had more than one.

Newspapers had first informed readers of important events. Radio had then made news immediate. Listeners heard wars as they happened. But television took news to an unimaginably higher level. Now the sights and sounds of history—from the moonwalk to the assassination of President John F. Kennedy to the Vietnam War—were experienced in living rooms.

Television changed the way people viewed everything from politics to sports. And it changed **journalism**. In the 1990s, the Cable News Network (CNN) started the first all-news network. Suddenly, news really was available at any hour of any day.

Cronkite and the nightly news

Television news began in 1948. It featured 10-minute reports before popular shows like *I Love Lucy*. Later, half-hour evening news shows were developed.

In 1962 a man named Walter Cronkite became the anchorman (lead reporter) of the CBS *Evening News*. He established himself as a fatherly figure. Viewers around the world looked to him for information and even advice. Cronkite became the most trusted person in the United States.

During the 1960s and 1970s, television news became big business. Each of the three major U.S. television networks—the Columbia Broadcasting System (CBS), the National Broadcasting Company (NBC), and the American Broadcasting Company (ABC)—developed massive news departments. Millions of viewers relied on these powerful networks for news coverage.

In the 1960s and 1970s, TV news anchorman Walter Cronkite was known as the most trusted person in America.

Television became central to major news developments. Presidents like John F. Kennedy became masters of using television coverage to announce major policies. And television also made people aware of the harsh realities of war. During the Vietnam War, viewers were shocked to see images of dead soldiers shipped home in body bags. These images stirred popular demands to end the war.

The rise of 24-hour news: CNN

During the 1960s and 1970s, television news stuck to a usual formula. Sometimes the major news networks might run a special report to cover a natural disaster or an election. Otherwise, news

shows used their regular evening timeslots and then "signed off," meaning they ended for the night and only updated the news again the next day.

All that changed on June 1, 1980, when U.S. millionaire and **media mogul** Ted Turner introduced the world's first 24-hour news channel. It was called the Cable News Network, or CNN. Before its first **broadcast**, Turner had proclaimed, "We won't be signing off until the world ends."

The network reached its heights during the 1991 Gulf War. Iraqi leader Saddam Hussein invaded neighboring Kuwait, spurring a U.S.-led attack on Baghdad. CNN was the first television crew broadcasting live from Iraq. CNN's reports were so accurate that top military leaders admitted they were getting much of their war information from the channel.

Other media companies recognized that the 24-hour format would work for different types of news. Thanks to CNN we now have specialty news channels such as the Entertainment and Sports Programming Network (ESPN), which covers sports, and E!, which focuses on celebrity gossip.

CNN was the most important television news innovation of its day. By 1985 CNN was in 30 million homes. Audiences were glued to its nonstop news coverage.

Fox News: Fair and balanced?

In 1996 an Australian media mogul named Rupert Murdoch launched a news channel to compete with CNN. He called it the Fox News Channel. Murdoch accused CNN of being **biased** to liberal causes. Fox's motto was "fair and balanced."

Rupert Murdoch launched Fox News to compete with CNN. Critics says his channel isn't "fair and balanced," as its motto states.

But critics claim Fox is anything but "fair and balanced." Many believe Fox is biased in favor of conservative causes and politicians. Former Democratic National Committee Chairman Howard Dean called Fox News a "right-wing [conservative] **propaganda** machine."

Fox's supporters say the station provides a home for viewers whose conservative beliefs are not reflected in other media. For example, a competing cable network called MSNBC is widely seen as having a liberal philosophy.

News or noise?

To some people, there is nothing wrong with news channels having political points of view. After all, even Benjamin Franklin's newspaper was biased. Supporters say cable channels spark spirited political debate.

But others see a danger in opinions masquerading as news. "Nothing about these stations raises the level of public discourse [discussion]," says New York University journalism professor Mark Rosen. "They aren't news. They are noise."

Think like a critic!
Keep these key hints in mind when watching television news:

Beware buzzwords
Compare how one channel reports a news story versus another channel. Do they use different buzzwords? Buzzwords are words used to make certain ideas seem either negative or positive. You can often tell which side reporters favor by listening for a buzzword. For example, when discussing abortion, do they say *pro-life* (a buzzword for people who oppose abortion) or *pro-choice* (a buzzword for people who support abortion rights)?

Keep it in perspective
Whose point of view does the story represent? In 2009, a Boston police officer had a confrontation with a black Harvard professor. Some news reports emphasized the officer's responsibility to keep the peace. Others noted that police abuse of minorities is all too common. An unbiased reporter must show both sides.

Cover me?
Whose opinion is being covered, or discussed, and how? Think about whether a reporter presents only one side of an issue. Did she interview people with different points of view? Did she give them equal time? Or was the coverage dominated by just one opinion? Remember: There are two sides to every story—and usually more!

Fair or foul? Spotting news bias
So, how do you know when a news report is fair, and when it is biased? Your best weapon is knowledge. If you keep up with current events, you can spot if **journalists** are reporting them fairly.

This is the BBC

The United States is not the only nation to pioneer 24-hour news. Today, in the United Kingdom, the BBC is the world's largest broadcasting news organization. It has a greater **global** reach than any other news service. The BBC has a news-gathering force of 2,000 journalists, and 70 bureaus based around the world.

The BBC is the world's largest broadcasting news organization, reaching 240 countries.

The BBC first broadcast television news in the 1930s. But BBC television was suspended in 1939 because of the war. The UK public then embraced television in 1953, when 27 million people watched live news reports on Queen Elizabeth II's coronation (crowning).

BBC critics take aim

By law, the BBC is required to be free from political and commercial (money-making) influence. BBC executives boast that they answer only to viewers and listeners. The network's well-known standards for journalism have earned it a reputation as one of the world's fairest news services.

But the network's independence has been **controversial**. The UK government has often accused the BBC of being sympathetic to the nation's enemies. During the Cold War, when democratic nations like the United Kingdom opposed communist countries like the

Soviet Union (now Russia), critics felt that it favored the Russians. During the Gulf War against Iraq, anti-BBC politicians labeled it the "Baghdad Broadcasting Corporation."

Still, a recent poll ranked the BBC as the world's "best and most trusted provider of news."

Headliners: Broadcasting legends

Here are a few of the biggest names in broadcasting history.

Huntley and Brinkley

Chet Huntley and David Brinkley hosted NBC's wildly popular evening news broadcast from 1956 to 1970. It was the highest-rated program on television and the first news program to be shown in color.

Pauline Frederick Robbins

Pauline Frederick Robbins opened the door for women to be taken seriously as journalists. Known as the "Voice of the United Nations," she covered foreign affairs for ABC for 7 years, NBC for 21 years, and National Public Radio (NPR) for 16 years, starting in the 1940s. She was also the first woman to moderate (oversee) a presidential debate and to win the prestigious Peabody Award for broadcasting.

David Frost

Known as "the Cronkite of Britain," David Frost is recognized as a great interviewer. He **scooped** all U.S. media in 1977 when he became the first to interview President Richard Nixon after he resigned.

Christiane Amanpour

The UK-born reporter Christiane Amanpour is the chief international correspondent for CNN. Television viewers have become accustomed to seeing Amanpour report from major crises in global hotspots like Iraq and Afghanistan. Amanpour helped disprove the myth that women cannot report from war zones.

Al Jazeera: The voice of the Middle East

Television stations in the United States and United Kingdom have earned their share of controversy. But no network has caused more controversy than the Middle Eastern station Al Jazeera.

Al Jazeera's name means "Island" in Arabic. To some people, Al Jazeera is the most hated station in the world. To others, it is the most trusted.

The Al Jazeera TV network is trusted by many Arab viewers as a more unbiased news source than western media.

The Middle East does not have a tradition of journalistic freedom. Experts say that state-run television in many Arab nations is heavily censored and biased toward governments. At the same time, many in the region distrust western media. They think that U.S. and UK stations are biased in favor of Israel and **broadcast** anti-Arab propaganda.

In 1996 Al Jazeera debuted from a studio in Qatar. It quickly gained a trustworthy reputation in the Arab world. Al Jazeera

broadcast the news that state-run television often banned. But it also allowed opposing views that seemed to be missing from U.S. and UK broadcasts.

Al Jazeera has rapidly expanded into a huge television and Internet network. It gained worldwide attention following the September 11, 2001, terrorist attacks when it was the first station to broadcast live from Afghanistan, where terrorists connected to the attacks were believed to have been trained. Stations like CNN and BBC often use Al Jazeera footage on their own airwaves.

A strained relationship

But the station continues to stir controversy in the West. It has angered U.S. leaders by broadcasting videos from Osama bin Laden, the mastermind of the September 11 attacks. Both Fox News Channel in the United States and *The Guardian* newspaper in the United Kingdom have accused Al Jazeera of showing videos of masked terrorists beheading western hostages. However, that charge has never been proven, and *The Guardian* had to apologize.

In 2003 Al Jazeera's office in Baghdad was hit by a U.S. missile, killing one of its reporters. This further strained its relationship with the West.

41

The News Net: How the Internet Is Changing Journalism

News has moved online. For better or worse, the Internet has become a powerful medium and changed the nature of journalism.

Early reporters like **muckraker** Upton Sinclair reached hundreds of people with newspaper and magazine articles. Radio pioneer Edward R. Murrow and television giant Walter Cronkite brought sounds and images into living rooms. CNN founder Ted Turner envisioned a 24-hours channel.

But none of them could have predicted what a UK computer scientist named Tim Berners-Lee started by accident in 1991: the Internet, a **global** information space accessible to anybody with a connected computer. Berners-Lee simply wanted to make it easier for researchers to share their work. He had no idea that he was about to start a new phase in **media** history.

With the Internet, almost anyone can now find the news they want—when they want it. With wireless technology, people in search of news do not even need a computer. Today, most news is also available on "smartphones" like iPhones and BlackBerries.

Problems and controversies

But the new media model is not perfect. Many people around the world do not have Internet access. In the United States, about half of all minorities and about half of older people are not wired to the Internet. And only 7 percent of Africa and just 19 percent of Asia offer widespread Internet access.

Internet **journalism** has been **controversial**, too. To some, it has ushered in a new age of participatory journalism. That means, thanks to the Internet, average people are not just reading the news. They can also post comments on it, and even report it themselves on **blogs**. Many people see this involvement of everyday people as a good thing.

But some people warn that bloggers are not a substitute for well-trained **journalists**. As we will see, posting news on the Internet does not make it true.

Blogs

What are blogs? Short for "weblogs," blogs are online journals, a space where people can write almost anything they want. Anyone with a computer, simple software, and Internet access can start one.

In 2003, three-quarters of Internet users had never read a "blog." At the time, there were about 1 million blogs around. Today, blogs are transforming journalism and politics. People who log on to the Internet can choose from about 100 million blogs worldwide—and counting.

Bloggers: The new reporters?

Many blogs are no more than diaries. But some bloggers have produced journalism and social commentary. Writing from all different political viewpoints, people use blogs to break news stories and fire-off political memos.

When Haiti was devastated by an earthquake in January 2010, citizen journalists took cell phone photos like this one to provide some of the first images of the tragedy.

Blogs can influence other media coverage by checking facts and adding details to reports seen in major media. For example, in 2004, bloggers found mistakes in a CBS story charging President George W. Bush with avoiding military service in the Vietnam War. It eventually led to the resignation of veteran journalist Dan Rather. Also, like **tabloids**, blogs often cover stories that other reporters ignore.

"Bloggers who practice journalism are journalists," says blogger Ana Marie Cox. "It's as simple as that." Proving the increasingly important role of blogs, bloggers like Matt Drudge and Arianna Huffington were among *Time* magazine's most influential people in 2006.

Citizen journalism

What is "**citizen journalism**"? It is exactly what it sounds like: ordinary people without professional journalism training using technology tools—from cell phones to Internet blogs—to report and write their own news, or to fact-check and comment on other media reports. Citizen journalists might blog about an accident they saw on the street. Or they might investigate a news article and post the mistakes they found. Others may snap a video of a police arrest and upload it on YouTube.

The terrorist attacks of September 11, 2001, were a turning point in citizen journalism. Many ordinary citizens became on-the-spot witnesses to the attacks. They took pictures with their cell phones and wrote their personal accounts on websites and early blogs. In many cases, these regular people provided more complete news coverage than professional journalists.

Standards and rights

Yet critics say blogs cannot always be trusted.

Just as with other kinds of news media, there are different kinds of news blogs with different kinds of standards. Some are written by reporters from newspapers or television channels. But some are written by self-proclaimed reporters and citizen journalists (see box on page 45). Too often, many argue, these non-professional journalists do not have training and are less careful about checking facts. Also, some bloggers may use their web space to advance their own **partisan** causes.

But blog supporters believe that mainstream reporters should not have the exclusive right to present a subject. They say everyday people know as much if not more than reporters alone and should contribute to coverage.

People who support blogs also point to the fact that blogs can be important tools in advancing human rights (see box at right).

Blogs are only becoming more popular with time. Over 77 percent of Web users around the world say they read blogs. Top blogs attract more than 3 million visitors a month.

Many bloggers in Iran helped to organize massive street protests following disputed elections in 2009.

Blogging for freedom

Blogs are not just for diaries and advancing political views. They can also be tools for global human rights activists.

Bloggers have become the Internet voice of **dissent** in countries that do not allow basic freedoms. Human rights activists say blogs are important **forums** to challenge injustices in ruthless governments around the world.

Bloggers in danger

Many nations try to block bloggers from reaching large audiences. Blogging in these places can be dangerous. Bloggers have been jailed for posting anti-government messages in countries such as Egypt, China, Libya, and Iran. In fact, the group Reporters Without Borders estimates that 151 bloggers were arrested around the world in 2009 for posting comments critical of their governments.

Blogging has become a popular forum for dissent in Iran. There are 46,000 bloggers in the country, including a large number of female bloggers. But the Iranian government has responded by arresting bloggers, including journalists from some of the few newspapers not run by the state. Some of the bloggers are reportedly being held in solitary confinement and tortured.

In Saudi Arabia, in 2007 a popular young blogger was arrested for insisting on democratic reforms. Fouad al-Farhan used his blog to campaign for the release of jailed Saudi liberals.

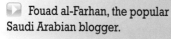 Fouad al-Farhan, the popular Saudi Arabian blogger.

Where to Now? The Future of News

A Twitter user sends a tweet from Westminster Abbey in London.

From the printing press to the Internet, the news **media** has seen incredible changes in the past few centuries. **Journalists** have adapted to change, moving from the page to the radio and television dials to the Internet.

So, what is next? Certainly the newspaper world is in trouble. Newspapers are losing **circulation**, advertising, and subscribers. Some have even had to shut down. Many have tried to gain a new identity online.

Internet sites and cable channels have stepped in, along with websites and **blogs**, to fill the space left by newspapers.

Many experts think the future of news will look much like the present, but more so. Blogs have popularized the idea of "**citizen journalism**," or ordinary people reporting their own stories on blogs or Internet sites. Hand-held devices like "smartphones" will let people read and report the news from virtually anywhere.

Experts say this is a hard concept for journalists to swallow. To some, citizen journalism is a dangerous next step from blogging. They imagine a media culture reporting unchecked rumors and gossip.

But others see potential in a news media that works with the public. Instead of news being reported by institutions like newspapers and television stations, experts see news models with everyday people participating in the media. In that wide-open model, citizens and reporters work together to ensure that the news is accurate and available to everyone.

One thing is certain: A new media model is coming. The ways we gather our news and the people who report it are bound to change yet again. But one thing will not change. The news will keep coming. Whether we read it in a newspaper, listen to it on a radio, or watch it on a television screen or computer, the news never stops.

Major Dates in Media History

1450 Johannes Gutenberg makes his first printing press. Suddenly books and news pamphlets can be printed more quickly. The cheap printing methods mean books are no longer a luxury for only the very rich.

1690 The first North American newspaper is printed. Called *Publick Occurrences Both Foreign and Domestick*, it lasts for only one issue.

1833 Benjamin Day opens the *New York Sun*, the first "**Penny Press**."

1922 The BBC is formed.

1932 Great Britain's King George V delivers his "Christmas message" over the radio for the first time.

1937 The German airship *Hindenburg* explodes, killing 35 passengers. The disaster is heard live across the world over the radio.

1939 BBC television **broadcasts** are suspended during World War II. They resume in 1946.

1945 There are fewer than 7,000 television sets in the United States and only nine stations on the air. Just seven years later, there will be televisions in 20 million homes.

1949 A U.S. law called the "Fairness Doctrine" requires stations to broadcast both sides of a **controversial** issue. It is **repealed** (undone) in 1987, allowing **partisan** talk shows on radio and television to present just one side of an argument.

1954 **Journalist** Edward R. Murrow uses his television show to speak out against Senator Joseph McCarthy. The Wisconsin senator famously accused many Americans of being communists. Murrow's show leads to McCarthy's downfall.

1960 For the first time, presidential debates are broadcast on television. More than 80 million people tune in to watch John F. Kennedy debate Richard Nixon. The handsome Kennedy benefits from the cameras and later defeats Nixon in the election.

1963 President Kennedy is shot in Dallas, Texas. Television coverage of the assassination and the funeral grip the nation and the world for days.

1969 U.S. astronaut Neil Armstrong takes humankind's first step on the Moon. The event is seen live by half a billion television viewers worldwide.

1970 The Teletext system is developed in the United Kingdom. The news-retrieval system lets users call up news, sports, and weather updates on their televisions.

1972 The first cable television system is launched. It is called Home Box Office (HBO). The Showtime cable network starts in 1978. ESPN makes its debut in 1979.

1980 U.S. **media mogul** Ted Turner creates CNN and broadcasts news 24 hours a day.

1987 Australian media mogul Rupert Murdoch launches the Fox News Channel.

1991 UK computer scientist Tim Berners-Lee puts the first website online.

1992 Nick News debuts on Nickelodeon. One of the first news shows aimed at kids, it is highly rated and wins praise for its political and economic reporting.

1996 The Arab news network Al Jazeera debuts from a studio in Qatar.

2001 The September 11 terrorist attacks usher in the age of **citizen journalism**, as ordinary citizens snap cell phone pictures and create **blog** coverage of the attacks.

2003 One million blogs are on the Internet.

2010 Experts estimate that as many as 100 million blogs exist.

Glossary

bias supporting one point of view, usually in an unfair way. Reporters try to avoid bias so that their stories are fair.

blog online journal

broadcast to transmit over the airwaves, like radio or television. Also refers to a radio or television program.

circulation number of readers a newspaper has, based on the amount of copies sold

citizen journalism when members of the public play an active role in collecting, reporting, analyzing, and spreading news and information

controversial causing a dispute or a strong disagreement between sides

corruption lack of integrity or honesty

crusade to strongly advocate in favor of something

dissent protesting to show disapproval, usually of an action or law

editor the person who determines the final content of a text, like a newspaper story

forum a public meeting or a place to discuss ideas

global involving the entire Earth

industry a commercial enterprise; a business

journalism the collecting, writing, editing and presenting of news, whether in newspapers, radios, TV, the Internet, or other forums

journalist a person who collects and writes stories or broadcasts news

libel false and damaging statement printed in a publication. It is intended to damage a person's reputation.

medium (plural: media) a means of communication, like radio and television, newspapers, and magazines

mogul an extremely powerful business person; also might be called a baron or tycoon

motto a saying that expresses a principle

muckraker crusading journalist who exposed corruption in the early 1900s

partisan supporting one point of view

"Penny Press" nickname for the cheap daily newspapers that were wildly popular in the 1830s. Costing just a penny, the publications drew readers with sensational stories, but also allowed ordinary people access to news coverage.

press a term for the news media

propaganda broadcast or printed material meant to influence public opinion

publisher the person or group who owns and prints a newspaper

repeal when something is undone

scandal a public controversy

scoop exclusive news item that is first reported by just one news organization

sensational intending to arouse great interest or controversy

tabloid type of newspaper known for combining news stories with gossip, often focusing on celebrities' personal lives. The term comes from the size of the publications' paper.

telegraph electric wire that carries messages in the same way as phone lines. In the early 1800s, it allowed news to quickly travel over long distances.

yellow journalism style of writing that stresses eye-catching headlines and sensational details over hard facts

Find Out More

Books

Adcock, Donald and Beth Pulver. *Information Literacy Skills* (series). Chicago, IL: Heinemann Library, 2009.

Bausum, Ann. *Muckrakers: How Ida Tarbell, Upton Sinclair, and Lincoln Steffens Helped Expose Scandal, Inspire Reform, and Invent Investigative Journalism*. Washington, DC: National Geographic, 2007.

Buell, Hal. *Moments: Pulitzer Prize–Winning Photographs*. New York, NY: Black Dog & Leventhal, 2002.

Cohen, Daniel. *Yellow Journalism: Scandal, Sensationalism, and Gossip in the Media*. Brookfield, CT.: Twenty-First Century, 2000.

Spinner, Jackie. *Tell Them I Didn't Cry: A Young Journalist's Story of Joy, Loss, and Survival in Iraq*. New York, NY: Scribner, 2006.

Sugarman, Sally. *If Kids Could Vote: Children, Democracy, and the Media*. Lanham, MD: Lexington, 2007.

Websites

"Don't Buy It: Get Media Smart"
http://pbskids.org/dontbuyit
This Public Broadcasting Service (PBS) site teaches media literacy for young people. It encourages teens to think critically about media and become smart consumers.

"Reporters Without Borders"
www.rsf.org
This nonprofit organization supports the rights of the press around the world. It supports journalists and tracks reporters who have been imprisoned, injured, or killed while covering stories.

News websites

"CNN"
www.cnn.com

"BBC"
http://news.bbc.co.uk

"Fox News Channel"
www.foxnews.com

"Nick News"
www.nick.com/nicknews

"Time for Kids"
www.timeforkids.com

Media watchdogs

"Media Matters for America"
http://mediamatters.org
A liberal media watchdog group that checks broadcasts for conservative bias.

"Media Research Center"
www.mrc.org
A conservative media watchdog group that checks broadcasts for liberal bias.

"Pew Research Center for the People and the Press"
http://people-press.org
This is an independent, nonpartisan public opinion research organization that studies attitudes toward politics, the press, and public policy issues.

Places to visit

The Newseum
555 Pennsylvania Ave., N.W.
Washington, D.C. 20001
Phone: 888/NEWSEUM (888/639-7386)
www.newseum.org
This Smithsonian museum is the world's only museum dedicated to the news. Exhibits combine five centuries of news history with up-to-the-second technology and hands-on exhibits.

Index